YOUR PASSPORT TO

PERU

by Ryan Gale

CONTENT CONSULTANT

José Antonio Mazzotti, PhD
Professor of Spanish Culture and Civilization
Professor of Latin American Studies
Department of Romance Studies
Tufts University

CAPSTONE PRESS
a capstone imprint

Capstone Captivate is published by Capstone Press, an imprint of Capstone.
1710 Roe Crest Drive
North Mankato, Minnesota 56003
www.capstonepub.com

Library of Congress Cataloging-in-Publication Data
Names: Gale, Ryan, author.
Title: Your passport to Peru / Ryan Gale.
Description: North Mankato : Capstone Press, [2021] | Series: World passport | Includes
    index. | Audience: Grades 4-6
Identifiers: LCCN 2020001028 (print) | LCCN 2020001029 (ebook) | ISBN 9781496684080 ;
    (hardcover) | ISBN 9781496688002 ; (paperback) | ISBN 9781496684592 ; (pdf)
Subjects: LCSH: Peru—Description and travel—Juvenile literature. | Peru—Social life and
    customs—Juvenile literature.
Classification: LCC F3408.5 .G35 2021 (print) | LCC F3408.5 (ebook) | DDC 985—dc23
LC record available at https://lccn.loc.gov/2020001028
LC ebook record available at https://lccn.loc.gov/2020001029

Image Credits
AP Images: Giancarlo Ávila/Grupo El Comercio, 13; iStockphoto: Nastasic, 10; Red Line
Editorial: 5; Shutterstock Images: Anton_Ivanov, 6, CP DC Press, 27, Filip Bjorkman, cover
(map), Izabela23, 9, J Duggan, 28, Jo Reason, 15, Mark Green, 22, Milton Rodriguez, cover
(bottom), Noradoa, 16, Peruvian Art, cover (flag), Skreidzeleu, 18, SL-Photography, 25,
studiolaska, 21
Design Elements: iStockphoto, Shutterstock Images

Editorial Credits
Editor: Jamie Hudalla; Designer: Colleen McLaren

Printed in the United States of America.
PA117

CONTENTS

Words in **bold** are in the glossary.

CHAPTER ONE

WELCOME TO PERU!

Stone **ruins** sit atop a rocky peak. Mountains and **tropical** forests surround the area. The ruins are part of the Inca city Machu Picchu. It is in southern Peru. More than 1 million people visit Machu Picchu each year. It is one of many historic sites in Peru.

Peru is the third-largest country in western South America. More than 31 million people live there. The **native** Inca people once ruled there. But the Spanish **colonized** the region in the 1500s. Both native and Spanish cultures have influenced Peru's buildings, foods, and traditions.

SIGHTS IN PERU

Peru has coastline and dry plains in the west. A tropical rain forest covers the east. The Andes Mountains lie in between.

MAP OF PERU

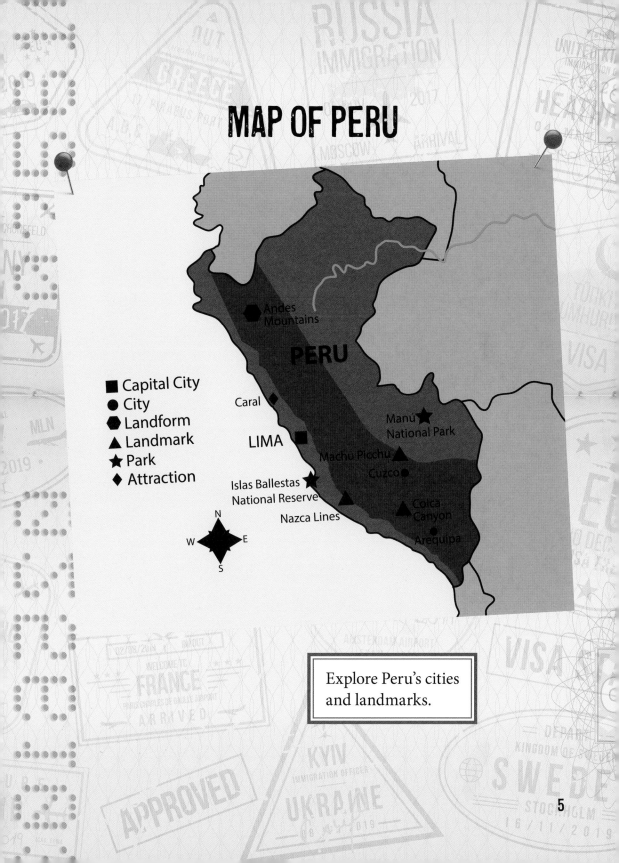

Map legend:
- ■ Capital City
- ● City
- ⬡ Landform
- ▲ Landmark
- ★ Park
- ◆ Attraction

Andes Mountains

PERU

Caral

LIMA

Manu National Park

Machu Picchu

Cuzco

Islas Ballestas National Reserve

Nazca Lines

Colca Canyon

Arequipa

N W E S

Explore Peru's cities and landmarks.

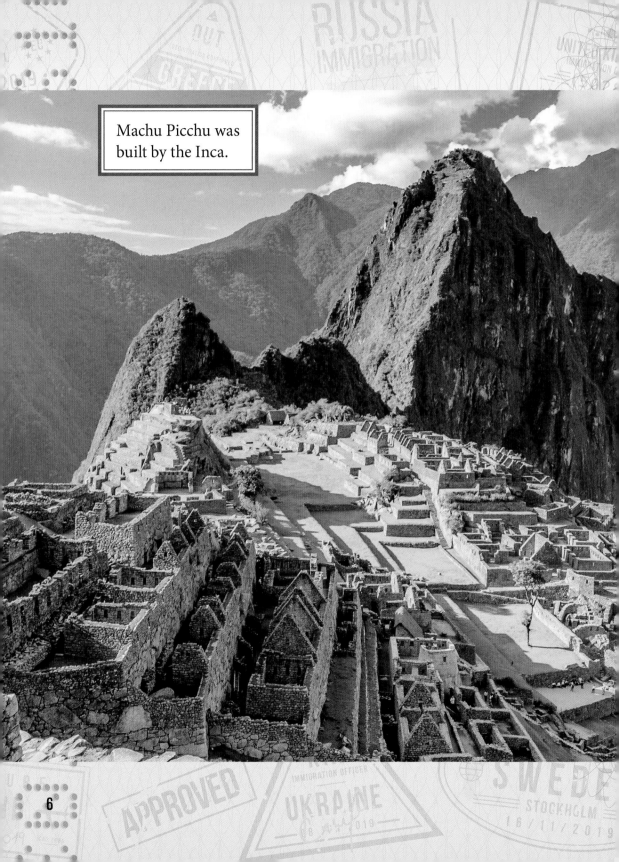

Machu Picchu was built by the Inca.

FACT FILE

NAME: .... REPUBLIC OF PERU
POPULATION: 31,914,989
LAND AREA: .... 798,596 SQUARE MILES (1,285,216 SQ KM)
CAPITAL: .... LIMA
MONEY: .... SOL
GOVERNMENT: .... DEMOCRATIC REPUBLIC
LANGUAGE: .... SPANISH, QUECHUA, AND AYMARA
GEOGRAPHY: Located in western South America, Peru is bordered by Ecuador, Colombia, Brazil, Bolivia, and Chile.
NATURAL RESOURCES: Peru has fish, coal, gas, wood, and gold.

Peru's West Coast brushes against the Pacific Ocean. These waters are home to dolphins, penguins, and many types of fish. Tourists can spot whales on whale-watching tours. They can also visit the beaches along the coast.

CHAPTER TWO

HISTORY OF PERU

People have lived in Peru for thousands of years. Cave paintings in southern Peru date back 7,000 years. The city of Caral is in western Peru. The Norte Chico, an ancient people, built it 5,000 years ago. It is one of the oldest cities in South America.

THE INCA

The Inca people ruled Peru between the 1100s and 1500s **CE**. They built hundreds of **pyramids**. Some may have been places to worship Inca gods. Rulers possibly used others to govern people. The Inca built roads. The roads helped them move goods and armies quickly. Pachacuti was the ninth Inca ruler. He used his armies to take control of other lands. The Inca **empire** became the largest in South America.

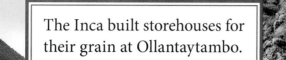

The Inca built storehouses for their grain at Ollantaytambo.

Conquistadors stole valuable items from the tombs in Huaca Rajada.

THE SPANISH

Spanish explorer Francisco Pizarro visited Peru in 1526. He saw a country rich in gold and silver. He returned in 1532 with a small army of Spanish soldiers called **conquistadors**. They destroyed the Inca empire.

FACT

The Inca had no alphabet. They spoke the Quechua language. It is still spoken in Peru today.

GUANO

Peru became famous for its guano in the 1840s. Guano is bird droppings. The islands off the coast of Peru used to be home to countless birds. Tons of guano had built up on the islands over hundreds of years. Guano contains nitrates, which help plants grow. People mined the guano. They shipped it to Europe and North America. Farmers used it to grow crops in areas with poor soil.

TIMELINE OF PERUVIAN HISTORY

2000s BCE: The city of Caral is built.

1100s CE: The Inca start ruling Peru.

1532: The Spanish conquer the Inca.

1780: People in Peru rebel against Spain.

1824: The people of Peru win independence from Spain.

1968–1975: Juan Velasco Alvarado becomes **dictator** of Peru.

1979: Peru creates a **constitution** that limits the president's power.

2018: Martín Vizcarra becomes president.

People from Spain colonized Peru after defeating the Inca. The Spanish forced native Peruvians to work in mines and give up their language and religion. Peruvians learned to speak Spanish. Many had to become Christians.

The people of Peru rebelled against Spain in 1780. But they were not able to win their freedom until 1824. Peru's leaders struggled to form a stable government.

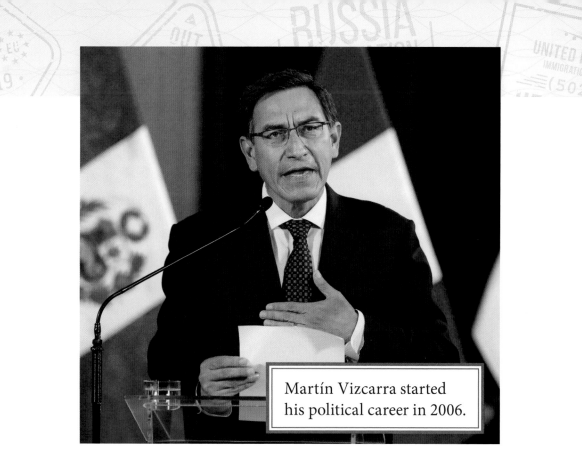

Martín Vizcarra started his political career in 2006.

A CHANGE IN POWER

In 1968, a military leader named Juan Velasco Alvarado took control. He became a dictator. Seven years later, other military commanders overthrew him. Peru created a new constitution in 1979. It limited the power of rulers. It also gave people more voting rights. Another constitution was created in 1993. Citizens now elect a president every five years. Martín Vizcarra became president in 2018.

CHAPTER THREE

EXPLORE PERU

Peru has amazing natural areas. The Amazon rain forest covers 60 percent of the country. It is home to many plants, such as orchids and lupuna trees. Animals such as spider monkeys and jaguars roam the forest. Some native peoples live there.

NATURAL SITES

The Amazon River begins in Peru. It flows into the Atlantic Ocean. The river is about 4,000 miles (6,400 kilometers) long. This makes it the second-longest river in the world.

Much of Peru's West Coast is desert. Peru's two largest cities are Lima and Arequipa. They are on the West Coast. The deserts spread to the foot of the Andes Mountains. The Andes stretch from the northwest to the southeast of Peru. The Andes is the longest mountain range in the world. People hike and climb in the mountains.

Jaguars roam the Amazon rain forest.

Rainbow Mountain is a part of the Andes Mountains.

People can explore Colca Canyon in the Andes. It plunges more than 10,000 feet (3,048 meters) deep. The Colca River flows along the bottom. Tourists raft down this river. Others hike or bike along the top of the canyon.

FACT

Peru has more than 1,800 species of birds.

WILDLIFE

People visit Peru's national parks to see wildlife. Manú National Park is Peru's largest national park. It includes parts of the Andes and Amazon rain forest. It has the most plant and animal species of any one place on Earth.

The Islas Ballestas National Reserve stretches across the southwestern coast of Peru. It is made up of several islands. Many sea creatures including sea lions and penguins live there. People can watch humpback whales swim along the northern coast of Peru between August and October. That is when the whales reach Peru from Antarctica, where they spend the summer.

FACT

The rain forest has many types of plants. Some can be used to treat illnesses. Scientists study the plants to find ones that might help people who are sick.

The Nazca Lines can be seen only from high in the air.

HISTORICAL SITES

Peru has famous historical sites that have become ruins. Machu Picchu is the most famous of these. The Inca built the city of Machu Picchu. They created it on top of a mountain. Historians think this may have helped protect the city from its enemies. Other ruins in Peru date back to a time before the Inca.

Peru is also famous for the Nazca Lines. These are drawings that the ancient Nazca people cut into the ground. Many are images of plants and animals. Some of them are very large. They can only be seen while flying above them. Some historians believe that the drawings may have been used to send messages to Nazca gods. Others think they were a form of calendar.

EXCITING CITIES

There is beautiful **architecture** in Peru's cities. Lima, Peru's capital, is known for its Spanish-style buildings. These buildings often feature **stucco** walls and tiled roofs. The Huaca Pucllana ruins are in Lima. This pyramid was built of clay bricks more than 1,000 years ago.

The city of Cuzco sits among the Andes Mountains. It was the capital of the Inca empire. Tourists can still see Inca ruins in Cuzco. The city is packed with food vendors, craft markets, and old Spanish churches.

CHAPTER FOUR

DAILY LIFE

Many Peruvians live and work in cities. There are usually more jobs in cities than in the countryside. Children between the ages of 7 and 16 go to school. Classes usually begin at 8:00 a.m. They end at 2:00 p.m.

People treat lunch as the biggest meal of the day. They often take a short nap after lunch. This is called a siesta. Many businesses close during lunch and siesta time. Businesses typically stay open until 8:00 or 9:00 p.m. This means people often eat dinner late in the evening.

LIFE IN THE COUNTRY

Many people who live in the country are farmers. They grow potatoes, corn, rice, and other crops. They also raise chickens, pigs, and other animals for food. Some people raise sheep, llamas, and alpacas for their wool. They sell the wool or use it to make clothing.

Many Peruvian schools require children to wear uniforms.

Quechua women often wear clothes with bright patterns.

A VARIETY OF FOODS

Peruvians eat different foods depending on where they live. People who live near the coast eat a lot of seafood. People who live in the highlands tend to eat meat, corn, and potatoes. Soups are popular in Peru. They are often made with spicy peppers. Dishes made with rice and quinoa are also popular.

LIMONADA

A lot of limes are grown in Peru. Drinks with lime in them, like *limonada*, are popular there. With the help of an adult, you can make limonada at home.

Limonada Ingredients:
- 2 limes quartered and seeds removed
- 8 cups of cold water
- ½ cup sugar
- Ice cubes

Limonada Instructions:

1. Place the limes, sugar, and four cups of water in a blender. Blend until the limes are crushed.
2. Strain the lime mixture and add the remaining four cups of water.
3. Serve with or without ice.

TRADITIONAL DRESS

Some of Peru's native people wear traditional clothing. This often includes coats made of brightly colored wool or cotton. They also wear knit hats and ponchos. Ponchos are a type of cloak often made from a blanket. They keep people warm high in the mountains, where it is cold.

FACT

Women living in the Andes Mountains wear traditional hats called *monteras*. The women decorate the hats with beads, flowers, and sequins.

CHAPTER FIVE

HOLIDAYS AND CELEBRATIONS

The people of Peru enjoy native and religious holidays. Peruvians celebrate Independence Day on July 28. Peru declared its freedom from Spain on that day in 1824. Some businesses and homes hang Peru's flag for the whole month of July.

The Inca Festival of the Sun is held in Cuzco. It honors the Inca sun god, Inti. It begins on June 24 and lasts an entire week. People recreate Inca ceremonies during this time. The ceremonies often include music and traditional costumes.

RELIGIOUS HOLIDAYS

About 60 percent of Peruvians are Catholic. Christmas and Easter are important holidays for Peruvian Catholics. The season of Carnival is also important.

People celebrate the Inca Festival of the Sun by dancing.

Carnival takes place in February or March. There are parades and parties. Carnival leads up to Lent. Lent is a period of 40 days. Many Catholics don't eat meat or certain other foods during this time.

CHAPTER SIX

SPORTS AND RECREATION

Soccer is the most popular sport in Peru. Peruvians call it football. Many children play soccer in school. The Estadio Monumental stadium in Lima is the largest soccer stadium in South America. It can hold more than 80,000 people. Volleyball and golf are also popular sports in Peru.

BULLFIGHTING

Bullfighting was once a big tradition in Peru. It is still practiced in some parts of the country. Bullfighting involves people called matadors. They wear bright costumes and carry swords or spears. They enter a ring with a bull and try to avoid being hit. The fight ends when the matadors kill the bull. But many people stopped watching bullfighting. It is harmful to animals.

Paolo Guerrero is considered one of Peru's best soccer players.

Many people enjoy hiking the Inca Trail.

THE GREAT OUTDOORS

There are many outdoor activities to enjoy in Peru. The Andes Mountains are popular with climbers. Many hike the Inca Trail. This 26-mile (42 km) trip starts outside of Cuzco and ends at Machu Picchu.

Some people like to ride dune buggies in the desert. Dune buggies are four-wheeled vehicles that climb mounds of sand. Sand surfing is a fun desert sport. People slide down a sand dune on a surfboard.

JUEGO DE SAPO

Sapo is a popular children's game in Peru. The game comes from an Inca legend about a magical sapo, or frog. People tossed pieces of gold at frogs. They believed that if the frog caught a piece of gold in its mouth, it would grant a wish. To play, you will need coins or tokens and a box with holes on the top. A toy frog with its mouth open must also be on the box.

1. Players take turns throwing coins at the box.
2. If a player tosses a coin in a hole, he or she gains a point.
3. If a player tosses a coin into the toy frog's mouth, he or she is an instant winner!

People also surf the waves on the Pacific Ocean. Some people go rafting on rivers in the Amazon rain forest. It is a good way to see animals and birds. From surfing dunes and waves to visiting ancient pyramids, Peru has activities for everyone to enjoy.

THE BIRTHPLACE OF SURFING

Some people think surfing began in Polynesia. Others think surfing started in Peru. Fishers in Peru have used small boats made of reeds for hundreds of years. Their boats look similar to surfboards. Ancient paintings and clay pots also show people riding waves. People in Peru still use reed boats for fishing and surfing.

GLOSSARY

architecture (AR-kuh-tek-chuhr) the style of buildings

colonized (KAH-luh-nized) settled in and took control of a foreign country

conquistadors (kon-KEYS-tuh-dors) 16th-century military leaders from Spain

constitution (kon-stuh-TOO-shun) the system of laws that state the rights of the people and the powers of the government

dictator (DIK-tay-tuhr) a leader who has complete control over a country

empire (EM-pire) a large area ruled by an emperor

native (NAY-tuhv) born in a particular country or place

pyramids (PIHR-uh-mids) structures with a square base and four triangular walls that meet in a point at the top

ruins (ROO-ins) the remains of an ancient structure

stucco (STUH-koh) a layer of cement and sand coating the outside of a wall

tropical (TRAH-puh-kuhl) a climate that is very hot and humid

READ MORE

Clapper, Nikki Bruno. *Let's Look at Peru*. Mankato, MN: Capstone Press, 2018.

Fullman, Joe. *3-D Explorer: Rain Forest*. San Diego, CA: Silver Dolphin Books, 2018.

Stine, Megan. *Where Is Machu Picchu?* New York: Penguin Workshop, 2018.

INTERNET SITES

DK Find Out!: Machu Picchu
https://www.dkfindout.com/us/history/incas/machu-picchu

National Geographic Kids: Peru
https://kids.nationalgeographic.com/explore/countries/peru

PBS LearningMedia: Virtual Field Trip Video: Coastal Peru
https://tpt.pbslearningmedia.org/resource/nature-works
-everywhere-vft-peru-clip/nature-works-everywhere-vft
-peru-clip

INDEX

OTHER BOOKS IN THIS SERIES

YOUR PASSPORT TO CHINA
YOUR PASSPORT TO ECUADOR
YOUR PASSPORT TO EL SALVADOR
YOUR PASSPORT TO ETHIOPIA
YOUR PASSPORT TO FRANCE
YOUR PASSPORT TO IRAN
YOUR PASSPORT TO KENYA
YOUR PASSPORT TO RUSSIA
YOUR PASSPORT TO SPAIN